THE OFFICIAL
MANCHESTER CITY
ANNUAL 2025

A Grange Publication

© 2024. Published by Grange Communications Ltd, Edinburgh, under licence from Manchester City Football Club. Printed in the EU.

Every effort has been made to ensure the accuracy of information within this publication but the publishers cannot be held responsible for any errors or omissions. Views expressed are those of the author and do not necessarily represent those of the publishers or the football club. All rights reserved.

Edited by David Clayton
Designed by Simon Thorley
Photographs © Man City and Getty Images

ISBN 978-1-915879-89-9

CONTENTS

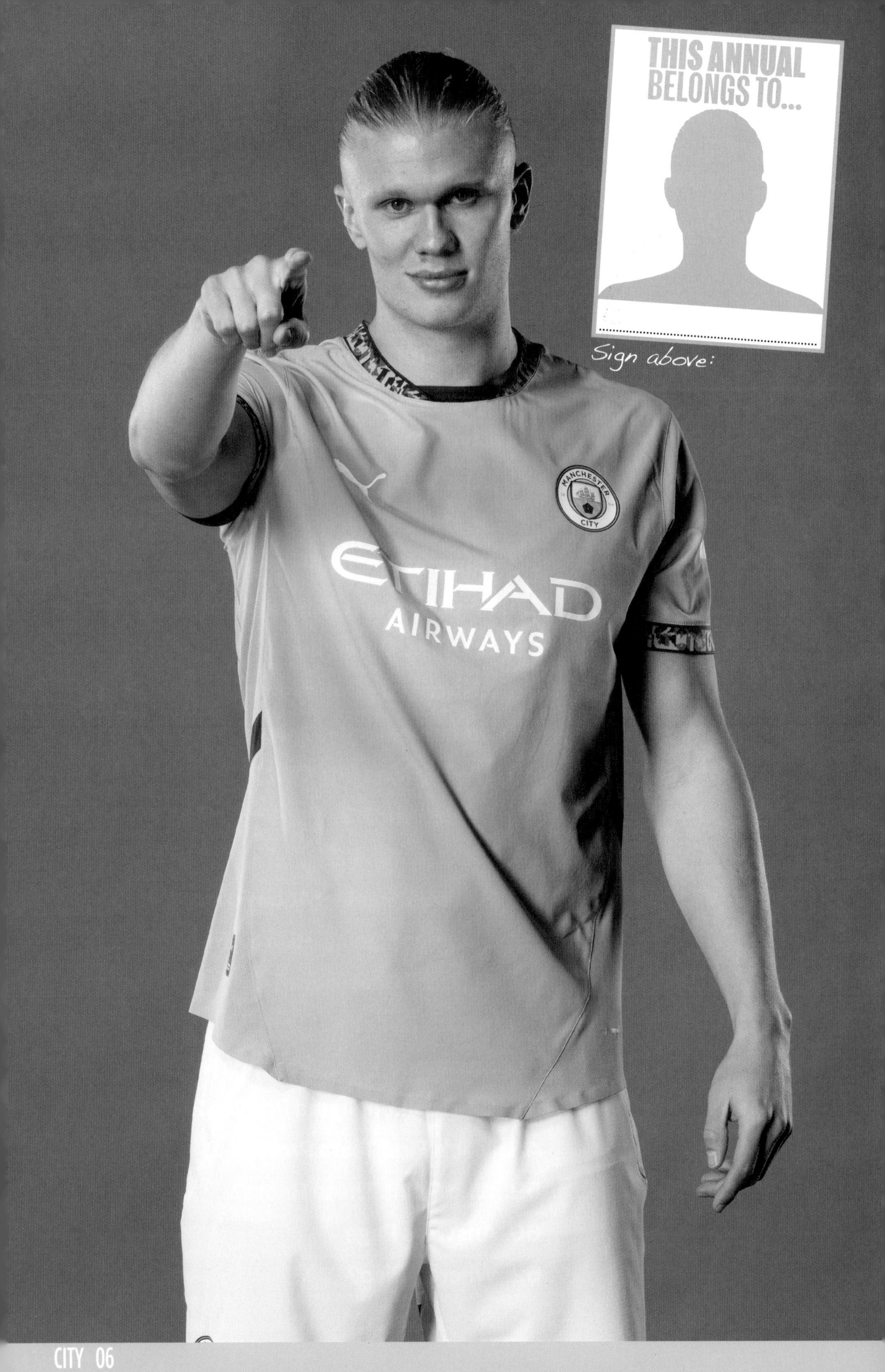

THIS ANNUAL BELONGS TO...

Sign above:

MEET CITY'S LATEST SIGNING – YOU!

Let's get to know all about you before we do anything else - fill in the form below and keep it safe for future years so you can see how many of your hopes and dreams came true – hopefully, all of them!

Age:

Team you play for now:

Trophies & competition I'd like to win the most:

3x stadiums I'd like to play at...

1)

2)

3)

Position:

Favourite squad number:

Player I'd most like to be like:

Design your boots:

Design a future City kit:

3x clubs I'd most like to score against (or save penalties if you're a keeper!)...

1)

2)

3)

Dream Manager...

YOUR PERSONAL PLAYER RATINGS:

Colour in the number of stars out of 5 you think matches your skill levels!

☆☆ ☆☆ ☆☆ ☆☆ ☆☆
☆ ☆ ☆ ☆ ☆

Speed: | *Shooting:* | *Passing:* | *Defending:* | *Team work:*

My best skill is:

Finally, we need your autograph to sign the contract:

Sign here: _____

STATS & FACTS 2023/2024!

It was another fantastic season – but what are the stats behind the campaign? Below are some of the best!

TROPHIES WON

PREMIER LEAGUE

FIFA CLUB WORLD CUP

UEFA SUPER CUP

FA YOUTH CUP

MOST ASSISTS (MEN)

KEVIN DE BRUYNE	17
JULIAN ALVAREZ	13
PHIL FODEN/RODRIGO	12

TOTAL GOALS SCORED

149

TOP SCORERS (MEN)

ERLING HAALAND	38
PHIL FODEN	27
JULIAN ALVAREZ	19

GOALS & ASSISTS (MEN)

ERLING HAALAND	38 + 6	=	44
PHIL FODEN	27 + 12	=	39
JULIAN ALVAREZ	19 + 13	=	32

(WOMEN)

TOP SCORERS

BUNNY SHAW	22
LAUREN HEMP	12
JILL ROORD/CHLOE KELLY	08

MOST ASSISTS

LAUREN HEMP	10
MARY FOWLER	08
CHLOE KELLY	07

GOALS & ASSISTS

BUNNY SHAW	22 + 05	=	27
LAUREN HEMP	12 + 10	=	22
CHLOE KELLY	08 + 07	=	15

FANTASTIC FODEN

PFA PLAYERS' PLAYER OF THE YEAR:

FANTASTIC FODEN!

He's one of our own – our No.47 playmaker is becoming not just one of the best in the Premier League, but also in Europe and the world.
Here are some of his incredible stats, facts and some of the things that have been said about our Phil...

PEP ON FODEN:

"[Can he be one of the greatest Manchester City players?] I don't know – this club has a long, long history. So you can't forget what happened with the players who played at Maine Road, like everyone knows. But if he continues his career until the end here at City and at the same level he can be one of the best, for sure."

SCORCHIO!

Foden's 2023/24 stats in all competitions are his best ever – he scored a career – high of 27 goals for City – 12 more than any previous season – and made twelve assists for his team-mates. Only Erling Haaland (38) scored more than the Stockport Iniesta.

TROPHY HUNTER!

Phil has won – get this – 16 major trophies with City! That's 6x Premier League, 1x UEFA Champions League, 2x FA Cup, 1x FIFA Club World Cup, 1x UEFA Super Cup, 2x FA Community Shield and 4x Carabao Cup triumphs. Incredible!

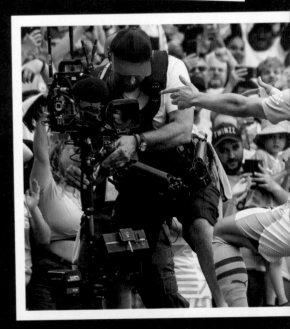

DID YOU KNOW?

Phil's favourite pastime is fishing! He loves the peace and tranquillity and often goes to the riverbank with his dad when he has a day off during the season.

FODEN ON FODEN

"I said at the start of the year I wanted to try to be one of the best players in our league. I think this season my game has come on loads, and I've performed really well. I've moved more centrally, where I see myself in the future. I'm just playing with freedom and playing with a smile on my face."

AWARDS HAT-TRICK

Foden's wonderful 2023/24 resulted in three major player awards. He was voted the Etihad Player of the Season by City fans for the first time, and he also won the prestigious Football Writers' Association Footballer of the Year and the Premier League Player of the Season.

MILESTONES LOOMING...

Phil should pass two notable milestones in 2024/25. He should pass the 300-game mark – he was on 270 going into the new season – and he needs just 13 more City goals to make it to 100. His average per game is approximately one goal every three matches.

KEVIN DE BRUYNE ON FODEN:

"Phil does what he does for six or seven years already and it's not like he's just come onto the scene. He's been doing this for years and helped us win titles. This year he went up a level."

DID YOU KNOW?

Phil was once a Manchester City ball boy at the Etihad Stadium and can be seen on some pictures behind the goal in his junior role.

WORDSEARCH#1

See how many City players' surnames you can find in our Wordsearch – remember, the words could be horizontal, vertical, or diagonal! There are 10 to find...

K	I	Z	R	O	D	R	I	G	O	U	B	B	G
O	D	Q	E	S	W	E	D	E	R	S	O	N	W
V	F	J	H	V	T	E	Q	F	B	U	V	B	Z
A	G	I	S	A	L	R	G	E	O	G	E	U	G
C	R	D	E	E	A	F	L	Y	X	D	O	O	V
I	E	D	O	K	U	L	C	E	E	T	E	C	A
C	A	T	B	F	R	Q	A	X	G	G	R	N	R
L	L	N	O	J	Y	W	N	N	C	C	A	H	D
E	I	W	W	A	L	K	E	R	D	B	S	X	I
A	S	C	K	O	Y	S	T	O	N	E	S	Q	O
L	H	A	O	F	G	L	M	F	K	G	C	L	L
Q	Y	D	B	I	Q	M	O	J	E	G	S	F	A
T	L	I	D	D	Z	M	M	M	E	V	J	F	F
E	D	E	P	B	N	E	C	C	I	F	H	S	V

GVARDIOL | FODEN | WALKER | EDERSON | RODRIGO
KOVACIC | STONES | DOKU | HAALAND | GREALISH

 ANSWERS ON PAGE 60/61

MANCHESTER CITY WOMEN'S QUIZ

Below are 10 multiple choice questions on our wonderful women's team – circle the box you think is correct and then see how many you've got right on pages 60&61.

1. How many WSL goals did Bunny Shaw score last season?
A. 15
B. 18
C. 21
D. 24

2. Which City player retired after the 2023/24 season?
A. Karen Bardsley
B. Demi Stokes
C. Ellen White
D. Steph Houghton

3. How many successive WSL wins did City achieve last season?
A. 12
B. 13
C. 14
D. 15

4. Which nation does Jill Roord represent?
A. Netherlands
B. France
C. Portugal
D. Belgium

5. Which team did Yui Hasegawa join City from?
A. Barcelona
B. West Ham
C. Liverpool
D. Wolfsburg

6. Goalkeeper Sandy MacIver changed the nation she represents – but which countries did she switch?
A.   Wales to England
B.   England to Northern Ireland
C.   England to Scotland
D.   Scotland to Wales

7. What did our home stadium for WSL games change its name to during 2023/24?
A. Joie Stadium
B. Mini Etihad Stadium
C. New Academy Stadium
D. Manchester City Women's Stadium

8. What was City's average crowd in 2023/24?
A. 4,500
B. 5,333
C. 6,112
D. 7,108

9. City were superb on the road last season – how many of our 11 games did we win away from home?
A. 10
B. 9
C. 8
D. 7

10. One team beat City both home and away in 2023/24 – who was it?
A. Chelsea
B. Arsenal
C. Manchester United
D. Liverpool

POINTS GUIDE:

How many did you score?
10 points – you are a genius!
7 to 9 points – fantastic work!
4 to 6 points – good effort!
0-3 points – must do your homework!

HISTORY MAKERS!

City created history by becoming the first team in England to win the Premier League title FOUR times in a row – here are the highlights of another wonderful season with our month-by-month look at what happened.

AUGUST ▶

City kicked off their Premier League defence with a convincing 3-0 win at Burnley with goals from Erling Haaland (2) and Rodrigo. Hard-fought league wins over Newcastle United and Sheffield United followed, with Julian Alvarez's goal beating the Magpies 1-0 and a late Rodrigo goal edging out Sheffield 2-1 at Bramall Lane.

Played: 3 Won: 3 Drawn: 0
Lost: 0 Goals for: 6
Goals against: 1 Points: 9

◀ SEPTEMBER

It was business as usual as City continued an impressive start. Fulham were thrashed 5-1 at the Etihad with Haaland scoring his first hat-trick of the season, before the champions won 3-1 away to West Ham United, with Jeremy Doku scoring his first goal for the Club. A 2-0 win over Nottingham Forest, however, came at a cost as Rodrigo was sent off after an altercation with Morgan Gibbs-White, resulting in a three-game ban.

Played: 3 Won: 3 Drawn: 0
Lost: 0 Goals for: 10
Goals against: 1 Points: 9

OCTOBER ▶

There was an early summit meeting with Arsenal at the Emirates for City whose 100% record was ended by the Gunners thanks to a deflected late Gabriel Martinelli strike. The Blues bounced back with a difficult 2-1 win over Brighton and a comprehensive 3-0 win over Manchester United at Old Trafford.

Played: 3 Won: 2 Drawn: 0
Lost: 1 Goals for: 5
Goals against: 2 Points: 6

NOVEMBER

November produced goals galore! Starting with a 6-1 win over Bournemouth, the Blues were then held in a thrilling 4-4 draw away to Chelsea, with Cole Palmer's added time penalty denying City. Worryingly, two more points were dropped at home to Liverpool in a 1-1 draw, with Trent Alexander-Arnold's late goal cancelling out Haaland's first-half goal.

**Played: 3 Won: 1 Drawn: 2
Lost: 0 Goals for: 11
Goals against: 6 Points: 5**

DECEMBER ▶

December proved to be another month of mixed fortunes for the Blues who dropped two points for a third game in succession. Despite leading twice, Dejan Kulusevski's 90th-minute equaliser earned Spurs a 3-3 draw at the Etihad. And six dropped points from three games became nine from 12 with a disappointing 1-0 defeat to Aston Villa. City were starting to lose ground in the title race, with Arsenal and Liverpool leading the way. The Blues were struggling to find their best form and a 2-1 win over Luton was a relief, but there was to be yet another setback as City squandered a 2-0 lead at home to Crystal Palace, drawing 2-2 at the Etihad. Just one win in six league games – was the title in danger of slipping away? A 3-1 win away to Everton relieved the pressure that was building, and a 2-0 win over Sheffield United ended 2023 with a high.

**Played: 6 Won: 3 Drawn: 2
Lost: 1 Goals for: 12
Goals against: 8 Points: 11**

◀ JANUARY

The return to fitness of Kevin De Bruyne gave the Blues a huge boost going into 2024, with the Belgian maestro returning to action in style, coming on when City trailed 2-1 away to Newcastle and scoring inside five minutes before assisting an added time winner for Oscar Bobb. That was followed by a 3-1 win over Burnley as the sky blue juggernaut shifted up a gear.

**Played: 2 Won: 2 Drawn: 0
Lost: 0 Goals for: 6
Goals against: 3 Points: 6**

HISTORY MAKERS!

FEBRUARY ▶

Recent history suggests this is the month when the 'Manchester City machine' really begins to motor – and with four Premier League wins out of five in February, who could argue? A superb Phil Foden hat-trick saw City win 3-1 at Brentford, followed by a 2-0 win at home to Everton, courtesy of a Haaland brace. Chelsea yet again proved stubborn opposition, holding City to a 1-1 draw at the Etihad. Then a hard-fought 1-0 home victory over Brentford was followed by an equally difficult 1-0 win away to improving Bournemouth as the Blues continued to find ways of getting over the line.

Played: 5 Won: 4 Drawn: 1
Lost: 0 Goals for: 8
Goals against: 2 Points: 13

Played: 3 Won: 1 Drawn: 2
Lost: 0 Goals for: 4
Goals against: 2 Points: 5

◀ MARCH

March was another unbeaten month for Pep Guardiola's side. City began with a 3-1 win over Manchester United at the Etihad – Phil Foden scoring a wonderful brace of goals - before we collected a valuable point away to Liverpool. March ended with what was dubbed as a potential title decider with Arsenal at the Etihad – the visitors would defend in numbers and leave with a 0-0 draw... but who would count the cost of those dropped points the most at the end of the season?

APRIL ▶

With a thrilling title race hotting up, there was no room for error in a busy April. City started by superbly dispatching Aston Villa 4-1 at the Etihad – inspired by a mesmeric Foden performance which saw the playmaker grab his second hat-trick of the campaign. The Blues then beat in-form Crystal Palace 4-2 at Selhurst Park, with De Bruyne in sparkling form. The Blues then effortlessly dispatched Luton 5-1 at the Etihad to keep the pressure on leaders Arsenal. The following day, both the Gunners and Liverpool were beaten at home by Villa and Palace respectively to blow the title race wide open. City swatted away Brighton 4-0 at the Amex Stadium followed by a nervy 2-0 win away to Nottingham Forest.

Played: 5 Won: 5 Drawn: 0 Lost: 0 Goals for: 19 Goals against: 4 Points: 15

MAY ▶

With the title destiny now in our own hands, City knew four more wins would guarantee a fourth successive top flight crown – something no other English men's club had ever achieved. Four goals from Haaland started May perfectly with a 5-1 win over Wolves before a tense trip to Craven Cottage to face Fulham. A tricky hurdle was comfortably overcome as City beat Marco Silva's team 4-0 leaving just six more points needed to win the league. Our game in hand over leaders Arsenal was away to Tottenham – and on a tense evening in North London, Haaland's tap-in on 51 minutes gave City a slender advantage before Ederson had to be subbed with an eye injury. Stefan Ortega Moreno came off the bench to replace the Brazilian and on 86 minutes, a Manu Akanji mistake let Son Heung-min through on goal – Ortega Moreno stood tall and made a magnificent save. Haaland then converted an added time penalty – his 38th goal of another memorable season – to seal a 2-0 win. West Ham were the only obstacle between the Blues and history and, though it wasn't as comfortable as everyone had hoped, a 3-1 win was secured and City were crowned champions.

Played: 4 Won: 4 Drawn: 0 Lost: 0 Goals for: 12 Goals against: 1 Points: 12

OVERALL VERDICT

(INCLUDING OTHER COMPS): Three trophies – the Premier League, FIFA Club World Cup and the UEFA Super Cup. We also competed in the Community Shield and FA Cup final and reached the Champions League quarter-finals -yet another impressive campaign by Pep's men!

SAVINHO

City's first major signing of the summer was Brazilian winger Savinho.

The exciting forward joined the Blues from Troyes after a wonderful season on loan with La Liga side Girona, who qualified for the Champions League for the first time in 2023/24.

But what can we expect from the new man? Here's a rundown of all you need to know...

Inspired by Mahrez

One of Savinho's idols is former City winger Riyad Mahrez and he admits some parts of his game were inspired by the Algerian. Savinho has taken the same shirt number Mahrez wore at City – No.26 – and if he can be half as successful as Mahrez was at City, he'll have done a great job!

Tractor Boy

Savinho spent his younger years living on his family's farm in rural Brazil. He did jobs around the farm and also milked cows when needed as there was no machinery to do this task – there are pictures of him smiling, sat on a stool with milk flowing into a bucket!

Rodeo star!

Savinho's family used to host rodeos on their farm and, as an accomplished horse rider, it's hard to imagine a young Savinho didn't take part! A rodeo is an exhibition involving horses and cowboys and can be very lively! Obviously, the injury risks mean it's not something he would be allowed to do once his football career took off, but before that, maybe he did!

Nutmeg king!

Savinho loves to knock the ball through a defender's legs whenever he gets the chance! It takes skill and timing to 'nutmeg' somebody and it can be a soul-destroying experience to have it done to you. The last City player to excel in this area was Leroy Sane.

Top dribbler!

City fans are in for a treat when Savinho plays. Predominantly a right winger, he has speed and agility to take on defenders, our new No.26 drops his shoulder and is away, beating one, two or sometimes three players on his thrilling drives towards goal. His 104 dribbles in La Liga while with Girona last season was the most in the division, with EURO 2024 star Nico Williams achieving 18 fewer!

La Liga Team of the Season

There's no doubt Savinho's influence on Girona's season was huge with the Brazilian scoring nine goals and claiming 10 assists. That form saw him named in the La Liga Team of the Season – no mean feat!

Brazilian favourites

Apart from Algeria captain Riyad Mahrez, Savinho had several Brazil stars as his idols growing up, The young winger particularly admired Ronaldinho, Ronaldo and Real Madrid's Rodrygo.

Wing Wizards

One thing City fans are really looking forward to seeing in 2024/25 is Savinho on one wing and Jeremy Doku on the other – both players are comfortable on either flank and their speed and trickery give the Blues a new attacking dimension that is likely to give many Premier League and Champions League defenders sleepless nights!

FACTFILE

Full name:
Sávio Moreira de Oliveira

Date of birth:
10 April 2004

Place of birth:
São Mateus, Brazil

Height:
5'9"

Position:
Winger

Former clubs:
Atlético Mineiro, Troyes, Jong PSV (loan), PSV (loan), Girona (loan)

GUESS WHO?

Can you figure out which City players are disguised below – there are clues if you look hard enough... but who are they?!

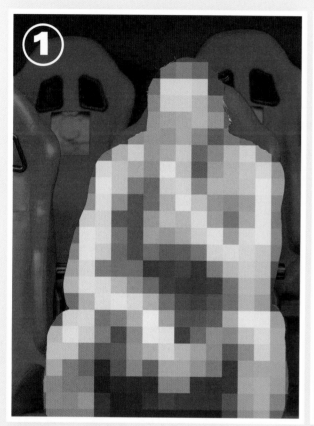

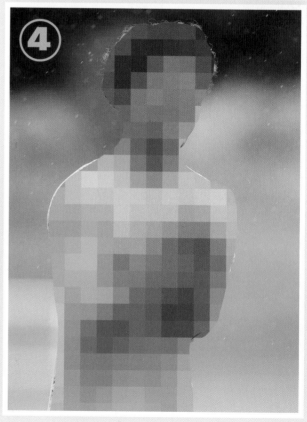

ANSWERS ON PAGE 60/6!

SPOT THE BALL#1

We've made the picture of Erling Haaland below into a grid so you can try and figure out where you think the ball is –good luck – it's there somewhere!

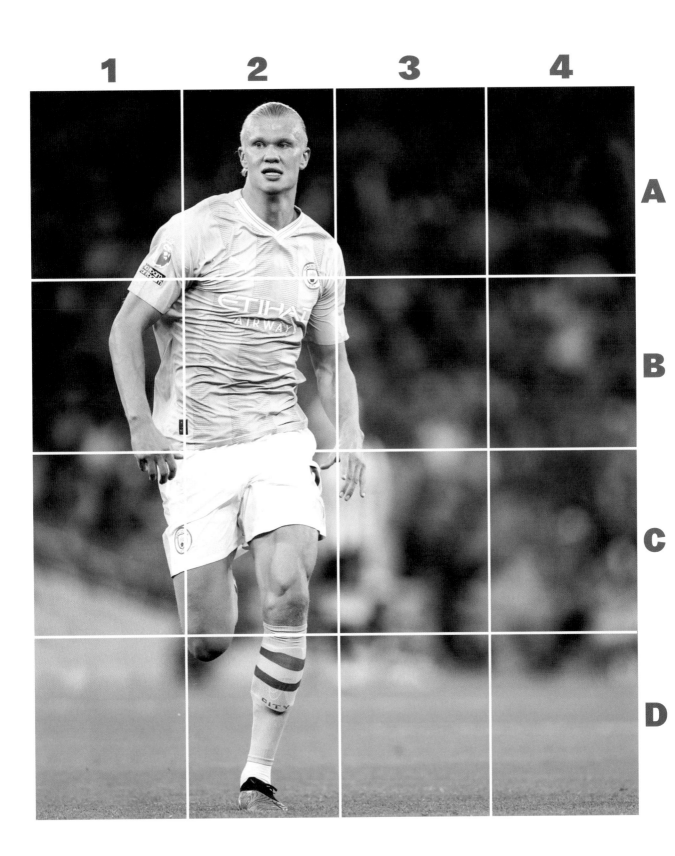

ANSWERS ON PAGE 60/61

HAALAND! HAALAND!
THE STORY SO FAR...
CRAZY STATS

Our Norwegian goal-scoring machine has been creating goal-scoring history as he keeps banging them in for City and Norway.
But his achievements so far in his career make his stats even more impressive – so here are some of the best so far!

▶ Haaland became the quickest player to 50 Premier League goals, taking just 48 matches to hit the half-century. Liverpool's Mo Salah needed 72 appearances.

▶ He has scored exactly two goals on the first matchday of his last four league seasons.

▶ The Norwegian has scored against all 22 opponents he faced in the Premier League!

▶ Haaland has so far scored six Premier League hat-tricks! Only seven players have ever scored more Premier League hat-tricks than Haaland, and they were: Sergio Aguero, Alan Shearer, Robbie Fowler, Thierry Henry, Harry Kane, Michael Owen and Wayne Rooney.

▶ The Norwegian was the first player in the Premier League to score hat-tricks in three successive home games and was the first Manchester City player to score a Manchester derby hat-trick since 1970- Phil Foden almost immediately joined him by scoring in the 6-3 win over United.

▶ Erling was the fastest player to ever score 25 goals under Pep Guardiola, doing so in 20 games to beat Lionel Messi (28), Samuel Eto'o (30), Sergio Aguero (35) and Thierry Henry (41).

▶ Erling broke the record for most goals in a single Premier League season in his debut campaign for Manchester City, scoring 36 goals in his 35 appearances.

▶ He broke the record for most goals in one season in all competitions by a Premier League player (52), comfortably surpassing Mo Salah in 2017/18 and Ruud van Nistelrooy in 2002/03 (both 44).

▶ Haaland is unsurprisingly the quickest player ever to reach three Premier League hat-tricks after getting there in eight games - and also the quickest player ever to reach four Premier League hat-tricks after getting there in 19 games. The previous record holder was Ruud van Nistelrooy, who took 65 games.

He was both the fastest and youngest player to reach 20 Champions League goals and at 20 years and 231 days old, Haaland was over a year younger than previous record-holder Kylian Mbappe as the youngest player to reach 20 Champions League goals.

Haaland has more Champions League knockout stage goals (14) than Neymar (13) managed in 32 games.

Erling Haaland, Lionel Messi and Luiz Adriano are the only players to score five goals in a Champions League game.

After just 33 caps, Haaland is second on the list of leading goal-scorers for the Norway men's national team with 30 goals and needs just four more to surpass Jorgen Juve's record of 33 -which has stood since before World War Two!

The Norwegian is the first player to score five goals in a single Champions League match and a single FA Cup match.

ERLING HAALAND HONOURS SO FAR:

Austrian Bundesliga: 2018/19, 2019/20
DFB-Pokal: 2020/21
Bundesliga Player of the Season: 2020/21
Bundesliga Player of the Month: Jan 2020, Nov 2020, Apr 2021, Aug 2021
Bundesliga Team of the Season: 2020/21, 2021/22
UEFA Champions League Squad of the Season: 2020/21
UEFA Champions League Forward of the Season: 2020/21
UEFA Champions League Top Goal-scorer: 2020/21
UEFA Nations League Top Goal-scorer: 2020/21
FIFA FIFPro World 11: 2021
Premier League Player of the Month: Aug 2022, Apr 2023
Premier League: 2022/23, 2023/24
FA Cup: 2022/23
FIFA Club World Cup: 2023
UEFA Super Cup: 2023
FA Community Shield: 2024
Champions League: 2022/23
European Golden Shoe: 2022/23
Premier League Golden Boot: 2022/23, 2023/24
Premier League Player of the Year: 2022/23
Premier League Young Player of the Year: 2022/23
Gerd Muller Trophy: 2023

CLUB STATS:

Bryne 2: 2015-16: 14 games, 18 goals
Bryne: 2016: 16 games, 0 goals
Molde 2: 2017: 4 games, 2 goals
Molde: 2017-18: 50 games, 20 goals
Red Bull Salzburg: 2018-20: 27 games, 29 goals
Borussia Dortmund: 2020-22: 89 games, 86 goals
Manchester City: 2022-24: 98 games, 90 goals
Total: 298 games, 245 goal

*stats up to date as of July 2024

FA COMMUNITY SHIELD CHAMPIONS!

Manchester City won the 2024 Community Shield after beating Manchester United on penalties after a 1-1 draw at Wembley Stadium.

Bernardo Silva's close-range header in the 89th minute cancelled out Alejandro Garnacho's opener which forced the showpiece to spot-kicks.

Kevin De Bruyne, Erling Haaland, Savinho, Ederson, Matheus Nunes, Ruben Dias and Manuel Akanji made no mistake from 12-yards and our goalkeeper saved Jadon Sancho's effort before Jonny Evans missed the target which saw us win 7-6 to kickstart the 2024/25 season in style.

It is the seventh time we've won the traditional curtain-raiser with the first time back in 1937 before subsequent victories in 1968, 1972, 2012, 2018 and 2019.

Pep Guardiola has now won the Community Shield on three occasions and now means he has won 18 trophies during his eight years at the Etihad.

He has now won a trophy in seven successive seasons for City.

SPOT THE DIFFERENCE

Time for some serious detective work! Taken in the dressing room after our FIFA Club World Cup win over Fluminense, study Picture A closely... and then look at Picture B – Picture B has SIX differences – can you spot them all? Circle each one you find and see if you can find them all...

PICTURE A

PICTURE B

ANSWERS ON PAGE 60/61

MANCHESTER CITY WOMEN

How Gareth Taylor's side came within a whisker of being crowned Women's Super League champions for only the second time...

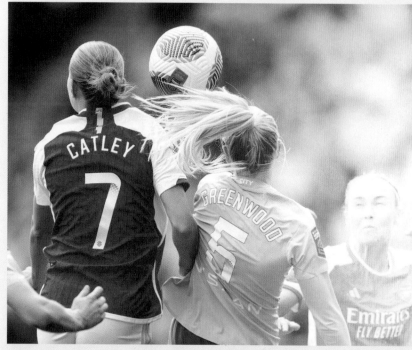

Goal difference agony!

City finished on the same points as Chelsea, but seven goals worse off on goal difference. It was a cruel blow for City who had led the table for several weeks following an amazing run of 14 WSL wins in succession, but with two games left, and leading 1-0 against Arsenal, the Gunners scored on 89 and 90+2 minutes to win 2-1 and take the title destiny out of our own hands.

Gunners jinx

City won 18 of 22 WSL games, drawing one and losing three times. Of those losses, one was a shock home defeat to Brighton – and the other two were against Arsenal. The Blues also scored in 21 of 22 WSL matches, with only a 0-1 loss to Brighton drawing a blank – and the Seagulls ended with the second-worst defensive record in the league!

Best defence

With just 15 WSL goals conceded, City's defence was the meanest in the league, keeping nine clean sheets out of 22 games. Only one team managed to score more than one goal against City in 2023/24 – and they did it twice. The team? Arsenal...

Shaw Shot!

Bunny Shaw scored 22 goals in 25 games for City in all competitions and her late season injury arguably cost City the WSL title as her goals and presence are crucial to the team. With 21 of her goals coming in the WSL, she won the Golden Boot for 2023/24 as well as being voted the WSL Player of the Season, the Manchester City Joie Player of the Season, and the Football Writers' Association Women's Footballer of the Year.

Golden Gloves!

Khiara Keating celebrated a wonderful first season with City, becoming the Club's No.1 and with nine clean sheets, Keating won the WSL Golden Glove award at the first time of asking!

The Incredibles

City enjoyed a fantastic run of WSL wins in 2023/24 – Gareth Taylor's side won 14 WSL matches on the bounce in the league over a period of six months to set a new Club record, scoring 48 goals and conceding only eight.

ILKAY GÜNDOĞAN

One of the surprise transfer deals of this or any other window was the return of former skipper Ilkay Gundogan.

The hugely popular German left the club in the summer of 2023 to join Barcelona but returned to the Etihad after just one year away.

He has agreed a one-year deal with the option for another year as he resumes life in sky blue.

One of Europe's best and most versatile midfielders, 'Gundo' can play a variety of roles for Pep Guardiola, able to operate as No.6, 8 or No.10.

He even spent one season often filling in the 'false 9' position and scoring 17 goals! Gundogan spent seven hugely successful seasons at the Etihad before moving to the La Liga side in June 2023, just 16 days after captaining City to an historic Treble thanks to victory over Inter in the Champions League final in Istanbul.

During his first stint at the Club, he won five Premier League titles, two FA Cups, four League Cups, two Community Shields and one Champions League, making 304 appearances and scoring 60 goals.

He made 51 appearances for Barcelona in all competitions and helped the Catalan giants finish second in La Liga.

Now he's looking to add yet more trophies to his sizeable collection! Ilkay has also taken the decisions to retire from international football, having won 82 caps for Germany.

On his return, he said: "My seven years at Manchester City were a time of pure contentment for me, both on and off the pitch.

"I grew as a person and a player, developed a special relationship with the City fans and enjoyed amazing success. It was an exceptional period in my life.

"To have the opportunity to return here means so much. And what can I say about my teammates here at City...they are world class footballers. I am genuinely delighted to have the chance to train and play alongside them."

Gundogan created many special memories during his first spell at City.

He will be forever remembered as the captain who wore the armband during the historic Treble-winning season of 2022/23 - something that no other City skipper had managed before. But his list of wonderful memories doesn't end there.

Who could forget his appearances as a sub on the final day of the 2021/22 season when he scored twice to help City complete a stunning turnaround from 2-0 down to secure a 3-2 win over Aston Villa and so seal the Premier League title.

And his spectacular goal after just 12 seconds in the 2023 FA Cup final against Manchester United – followed by another volley that won the game 2-1 – will live long in the memory.

His return will be a huge boost to the dressing room, where he was one of the most respected players at the Club.
Guardiola once said of him, "When he talks, everyone listens."

Gundo will provide cover for Rodrigo when needed, support Kevin De Bruyne, Phil Foden and Mateo Kovacic and also help feed Erling Haaland with clever passes and crosses.

It was a deal that was simply too good to turn down for City and our returning German star will wear the No.19 shirt vacated by Julian Alvarez – he did wear the No.8 jersey during his first spell, but this has since been taken by Mateo Kovacic.

"It feels so good to be home," said Ilkay after re-joining the Blues.

THE BIG 2025
Man City Quiz

You will need all your City knowledge to crack our Big City quiz which is tougher than ever! See how many you get right and then check your score and your rating – the answers are on page 60 & 61...but no cheating!

01 Who was City's men's top scorer (all comps) in 2023/24?

02 Who did City beat City in the final of the FIFA Club World Cup?

03 Who scored in the UEFA Super Cup against Sevilla and the FA Community Shield against Arsenal – before leaving for Chelsea?

04 How many goals did City score in total during 2023/24? *A) 145 B) 149 C) 155*

05 Who was City Women's top scorer for 2023/24?

06 Which team did Erling Haaland score five goals in one game against in 2023/24? *A) Luton Town B) Bournemouth C) Fulham*

07 What nationality is City Women coach Gareth Taylor? *A) English B) Welsh C) Scottish*

08 True or false? The last three times City have been knocked out of the Champions League by Real Madrid, the Spanish side have gone on to win the competition.

08

Who is this pictured above?

True or false? Jack Grealish and Declan Rice both played for Republic of Ireland before switching to England.

11 Who knocked City out of the Carabao Cup in 2023/24?

12 Who did City beat to win the FA Youth Cup?

13 How many City players competed at EURO 2024?

14 Which English city was Erling Haaland born in?

15 Which club did City sign Josko Gvardiol from?

16 True or false? City lost five games in all competitions during 2023/24 – all by a one-goal margin.

17 How many penalty shoot-outs did City win out of three in 2023/24?

18 Who is this below?

19 Which of these clubs did NOT play City in the 2023/24 Champions League? *A) RB Leipzig B) Real Sociedad C) FC Copenhagen*

20 Who was voted the men's Etihad Player of the Season for 2023/24?

21 Who were the only Premier League side to stop City scoring both home and away in 2023/24?

22 Which former assistant to Pep Guardiola became Chelsea boss in June 2024?

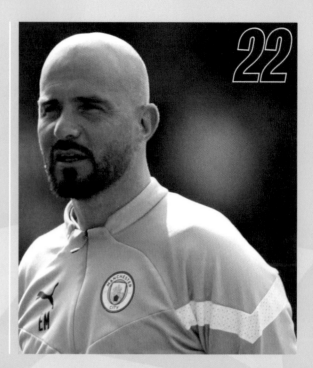

23 Which City midfielder scored his 100th goal for the club in 2023/24? *A) Phil Foden B) Bernardo Silva C) Kevin De Bruyne*

24 How many top flight titles have City now won (including pre-Premier League)? *A) 5 B) 8 C) 10*

25 How many points did City win the title by? *A) 1 B) 2 C) 3*

26 How many trophies has Pep Guardiola won at City? *A) 18 B) 15 C) 13*

27 Who is this above?

28 What is the name of City's former stadium (1923 to 2003) ?

29 Solve this anagram to discover a City player: HEN JOTS SON

30 What does Julian Alvarez's nickname La Araña mean in English?

36 What did Matheus Nunes, Ruben Dias and Kyle Walker all NOT do in 2023/24?

37 Who scored a goal in our first and last Premier League games of 2023/24?

38 Which Caribbean country does Bunny Shaw represent?

39 Which club did City sign Kyle Walker from?

40 How many hat-tricks did Phil Foden score in 2023/24? A) 1 B) 2 C) 3

31 Which German club did Manuel Akanji join City from?

32 Who wears No.8 for City's men's team?

33 Who wears No.8 for City's women's team?

34 True or false – both City's games against Liverpool in 2023/24 ended 2-2.

35 Two City players were shown red cards in 2023/24 – who were they?

Score: *One point for each correct question...*

0-9 points	Stay behind and do your City homework!
10-19 points	Great effort! Well done!
20-29 points	Fantastic! Your City knowledge is impressive!
30-40 points	Amazing! You are a City know-it-all!

GUESS WHO#2

Here's your second helping of detective work to figure out which four City players are disguised below – the pictures were all taken after the 2023/24 Premier League trophy celebrations... but who are they?!

ANSWERS ON PAGE 60/61

WORDSEARCH#2

There are 10 of our Manchester City Women players' surnames hidden in the wordsearch below – horizontal, vertical, or diagonal... see how many you can find!

Y	B	S	F	J	T	T	F	V	K	E	L	L	Y
U	G	Y	T	D	J	G	Z	P	E	X	R	T	H
Z	P	Z	H	R	C	V	V	A	A	A	C	O	M
G	N	M	Z	A	O	F	Y	R	T	Y	A	W	U
Q	F	Q	Q	A	S	O	A	K	I	I	S	B	G
Q	G	G	J	T	K	E	R	Z	N	U	P	Y	J
U	E	B	R	O	G	A	G	D	G	R	A	X	M
P	A	E	S	E	M	P	I	A	B	Y	R	V	T
R	F	O	W	L	E	R	Y	N	W	P	I	H	W
A	D	O	A	Y	K	N	K	R	N	A	J	H	D
G	A	C	L	W	Z	M	W	T	W	U	E	E	M
D	J	C	M	S	W	K	H	O	I	O	W	M	V
O	V	W	X	E	P	X	C	F	O	B	S	P	E
Y	C	P	S	H	A	W	X	H	A	D	F	W	Z

ROORD | KELLY | SHAW | KEATING | HASEGAWA
HEMP | PARK | GREENWOOD | FOWLER | CASPARIJ

SUMMER SIGNING
AOBA FUJINO

Aoba Fujino became City's third Japanese international when she signed a three-year deal in the summer.

The 20-year-old forward took part in the Paris Olympics and will wear the No. 20 shirt. So, what can we expect from our new arrival? Fujino is a two-time winner of the WE League Valuable Player Award during her three seasons with Tokyo Verdy Beleza, who she played 51 games for, scoring 24 goals and providing 17 assists.

She was a rising star at the 2023 World Cup, where she became her nation's youngest ever goal scorer in the tournament.

The goal that saw her claim that impressive record, in a 2-0 win over Costa Rica, was the product of an outstanding piece of individual brilliance that many believed was evidence of the talent and ability of a future star.

Her assets include tenacity, a low centre of gravity, close control and the ability to score special goals.

She also had a starring role in the Under-20 World Cup, where Japan finished runners up in 2022.

Despite her diminutive stature, the forward knows how to keep hold of the ball, aided by tight control, clever movement and a sharp turn of speed over short distances.

Definitely a player who will get City fans off their seats, she joins fan favourite Yui Hasegawa and our other new Japan star Risa Shimizu at the Joie Stadium for what looks set to be an exciting season!

SUMMER SIGNING
RISA SHIMIZU

Japanese defender Risa Shimizu joined City ahead of the Olympic Games in Paris.

The 28-year-old arrives with Women's Super League experience having previously played for West Ham United last season.

Before her switch to West Ham, she moved to Yokohama during her childhood and shortly joined local team FC Susukino Ladies ahead of joining Tokyo Verdy Beleza in 2009.

Due to her outstanding ability, she was fast-tracked into their first team at the age of 17 in 2013 and established herself in their starting XI before enjoying a trophy-laden spell in her homeland.

After fully settling in England during her time in London, the full-back is certainly ready to operate at the sport's elite level and she will provide quality and competition to the excellent Kerstin Casparij as we compete on four fronts in 2024/25 – including the UEFA Champions League.

Shimizu has signed a three-year deal that will keep her at the Joie Stadium until the summer of 2027.

Shimizu is a confident and forward-thinking full-back who moved to the WSL in 2022 where she made 44 appearances in two seasons with the Hammers, scoring one goal.

The Japan international will wear the No 2 shirt for City and was on 79 caps for her country before the start of the 2024/25 campaign.

Since her international debut in 2017, she has featured at the 2020 Tokyo and 2024 Paris Olympics along with the FIFA Women's World Cup in 2019 and 2023.

MYSTERY GOAL SCORER!

We've disguised four goal scorers in the pictures below – can you figure out who they are? Maybe their celebration might give the game away – or then again, maybe not!

ANSWERS ON PAGE 60/61

TRUE OF FALSE?

This is a simple game with only two possible answers – true or false. See if you can correctly guess all 10!

1 BUNNY SHAW IS SCARED OF RABBITS
TRUE OR FALSE?

2 MANUEL AKANJI IS CONSIDERED SOMETHING OF A MATHEMATICAL GENIUS
TRUE OR FALSE?

3 CITY KEEPER KHIARA KEATING REPRESENTS WALES AT INTERNATIONAL LEVEL
TRUE OR FALSE?

4 THE ETIHAD STADIUM WAS OPENED AS A FOOTBALL VENUE IN 2003
TRUE OR FALSE?

5 RUBEN DIAS ONCE SERVED IN THE PORTUGUESE ARMY
TRUE OR FALSE?

6 KYLE WALKER IS A SHEFFIELD WEDNESDAY FAN
TRUE OR FALSE?

7 ERLING HAALAND ONCE WENT AN ENTIRE SEASON WITHOUT SCORING
TRUE OR FALSE?

8 *TRUE OR FALSE?* MATHEUS NUNES ONCE WORKED IN A BAKERY

9 *TRUE OR FALSE?* NATHAN AKE IS A GREAT PIANO PLAYER

10 *TRUE OR FALSE?* RODRIGO HAS REPRESENTED SPAIN AT BASKETBALL

ANSWERS ON PAGE 60/61

VIVIANNE MIEDEMA

Meet our new Dutch goal-scoring machine!
One of the WSL signings of the summer, Vivianne Miedema joined City after penning a three-year deal..

The 27-year-old forward spent seven seasons with Arsenal, breaking and setting numerous records along the way.

The Dutch international is at the peak of her powers and, alongside Bunny Shaw, will form one of the most feared attacking partnerships anywhere in the world.

Miedema is the Barclays Women's Super League's record goal scorer having bagged 80 in 106 starts for the Gunners and 125 in 172 games in all competitions.

She has also scored 95 goals in 118 games for Netherlands, as well as a club career tally of 260 goals in 335 matches.

Add her club and country figures together and you have 345 goals in 453 matches!

Miedema will wear the No.6 shirt for City and joins fellow Dutch international team-mates Jill Roord and Kerstin Casparij.

However, it's not only goals that our new forward will provide in the coming years.

Unselfish and intelligent, Miedema is in many ways the perfect attack-minded player. She was the first player in WSL history to register 100 goal contributions, managing this incredible feat in only 83 appearances after scoring 70 and making another 30 for her team-mates.

In fact, she describes herself more as an attacking midfielder, able to score and create from anywhere in the final third and immediately drawing comparisons with similar players such as Kevin De Bruyne from our men's team (in case you didn't know!).

An exciting signing and one that City hope will end up resulting in more silverware at home and abroad in the coming seasons.

In her own words: "The reason I chose City is because they have the same ambitions as me. They want to win the league and titles.

"Looking to the future, I've always said I want to play with best players in the world and I think City have got that.

"I think and hope my best years are still to come. I hope I'm going to be able to help the team as much as I can do.

"I am just really excited to be part of the team and for the girls to hopefully help me and get me back to my best. If I get back to my best again then we can achieve really nice things together.

"I do think this is the place to be right now. In the end, it was an easy choice for me. I want to challenge myself every day in training, but also every single week in the games we play."

Gareth Taylor's view: "We're really looking forward to welcoming Viv to City and seeing her flourish over the next three years.

"Our ambition is to compete on the highest stage and for the highest honours, and Viv is aligned to this desire.

"She's a top talent that I'm excited to work with as she's a player I've always admired. Viv will be a real asset to the team."

Bayern Munich [2014-17]
Bundesliga: 2014/15, 2015/16

Arsenal [2017-2024]
FA WSL: 2018/19
FA WSL Cup/FA Women's League Cup:
2017/18, 2022/23, 2023/24

Netherlands [2013-present]
UEFA Women's Championship: 2017

Individual
FA WSL Golden Boot: 2018/19, 2019/20
FIFA Women's World Cup All-Star Squad: 2019
PFA Women's Players' Player of the Year: 2018/19
FWA Women's Footballer of Year: 2019/20
FIFA FIFPro Women's World11: 2020, 2021
BBC Women's Footballer of the Year: 2021
PFA Team of the Year: 2018/19, 2019/20, 2021/22

NAME: KHIARA KEATING
COUNTRY: ENGLAND
POSITION: GOALKEEPER
SQUAD NUMBER: 35
DATE OF BIRTH:
27/06/2004

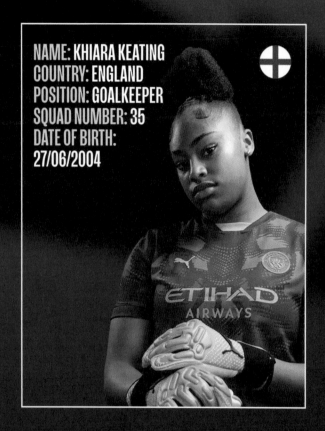

NAME: AYAKA YAMASHITA
COUNTRY: JAPAN
POSITION: GOALKEEPER
SQUAD NUMBER: 31
DATE OF BIRTH:
29/09/1995

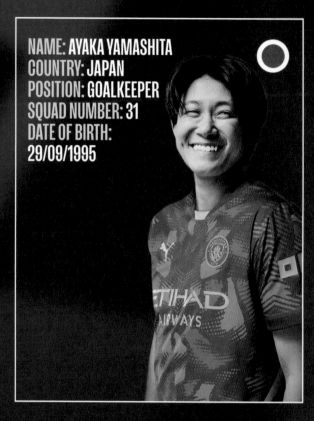

NAME: SANDY MACIVER
COUNTRY: SCOTLAND
POSITION: GOALKEEPER
SQUAD NUMBER: 22
DATE OF BIRTH:
18/06/1998

NAME: LAIA ALEIXANDRI
COUNTRY: SPAIN
POSITION: DEFENDER
SQUAD NUMBER: 4
DATE OF BIRTH:
25/08/2000

NAME: KERSTIN CASPARIJ
COUNTRY: NETHERLANDS
POSITION: DEFENDER
SQUAD NUMBER: 18
DATE OF BIRTH:
19/08/2000

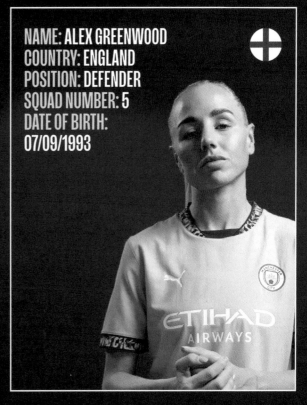

NAME: ALEX GREENWOOD
COUNTRY: ENGLAND
POSITION: DEFENDER
SQUAD NUMBER: 5
DATE OF BIRTH:
07/09/1993

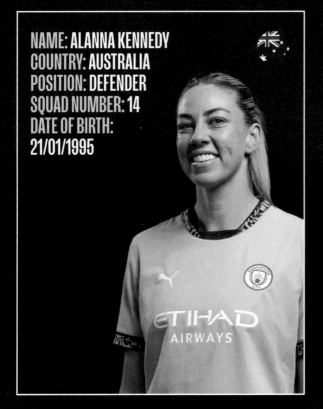

NAME: ALANNA KENNEDY
COUNTRY: AUSTRALIA
POSITION: DEFENDER
SQUAD NUMBER: 14
DATE OF BIRTH:
21/01/1995

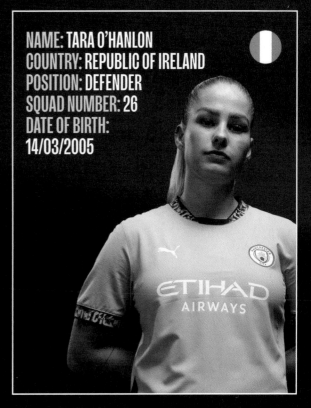

NAME: TARA O'HANLON
COUNTRY: REPUBLIC OF IRELAND
POSITION: DEFENDER
SQUAD NUMBER: 26
DATE OF BIRTH:
14/03/2005

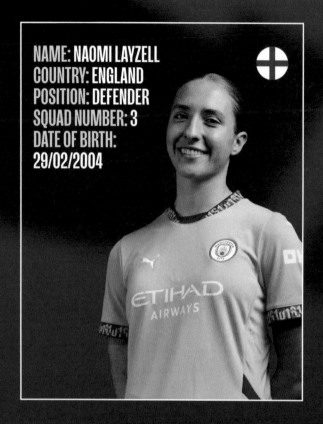

NAME: NAOMI LAYZELL
COUNTRY: ENGLAND
POSITION: DEFENDER
SQUAD NUMBER: 3
DATE OF BIRTH: 29/02/2004

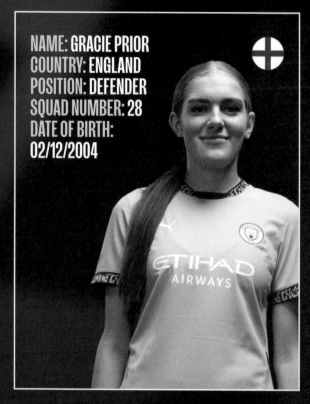

NAME: GRACIE PRIOR
COUNTRY: ENGLAND
POSITION: DEFENDER
SQUAD NUMBER: 28
DATE OF BIRTH: 02/12/2004

NAME: RISA SHIMIZU
COUNTRY: JAPAN
POSITION: DEFENDER
SQUAD NUMBER: 2
DATE OF BIRTH: 15/06/1996

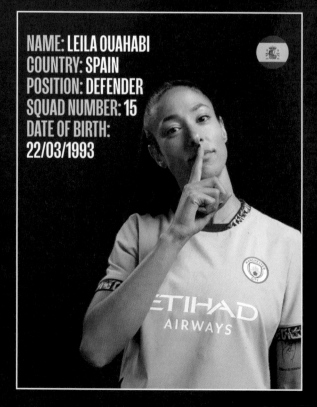

NAME: LEILA OUAHABI
COUNTRY: SPAIN
POSITION: DEFENDER
SQUAD NUMBER: 15
DATE OF BIRTH: 22/03/1993

NAME: **YUI HASEGAWA**
COUNTRY: **JAPAN**
POSITION: **MIDFIELDER**
SQUAD NUMBER: **25**
DATE OF BIRTH:
29/01/1997

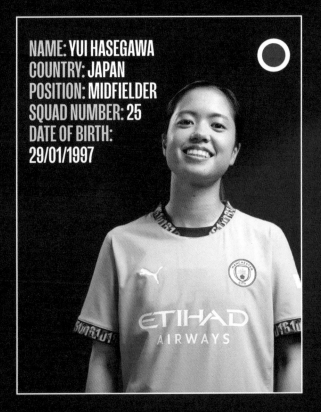

NAME: **LAURA BLINDKILDE BROWN**
COUNTRY: **ENGLAND**
POSITION: **MIDFIELDER**
SQUAD NUMBER: **19**
DATE OF BIRTH:
09/12/2003

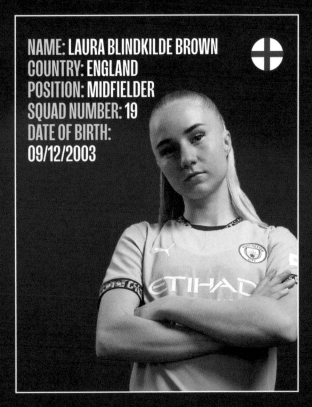

NAME: **LAURA COOMBS**
COUNTRY: **ENGLAND**
POSITION: **MIDFIELDER**
SQUAD NUMBER: **7**
DATE OF BIRTH:
29/01/1991

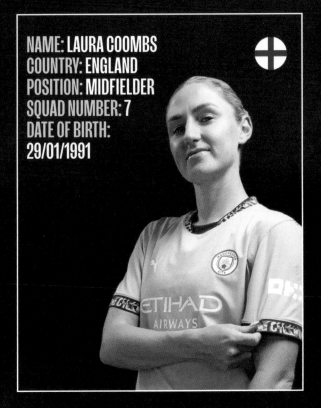

NAME: **JILL ROORD**
COUNTRY: **NETHERLANDS**
POSITION: **MIDFIELDER**
SQUAD NUMBER: **10**
DATE OF BIRTH:
22/04/1997

NAME: POPPY PRITCHARD
COUNTRY: ENGLAND
POSITION: FORWARD
SQUAD NUMBER: 17
DATE OF BIRTH:
03/12/2005

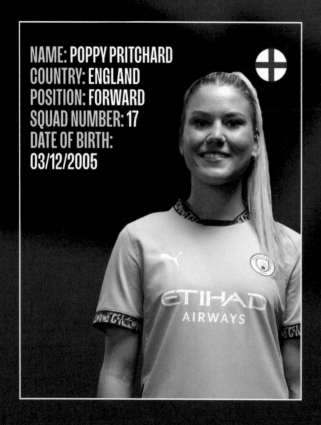

NAME: CHLOE KELLY
COUNTRY: ENGLAND
POSITION: FORWARD
SQUAD NUMBER: 9
DATE OF BIRTH:
15/01/1998

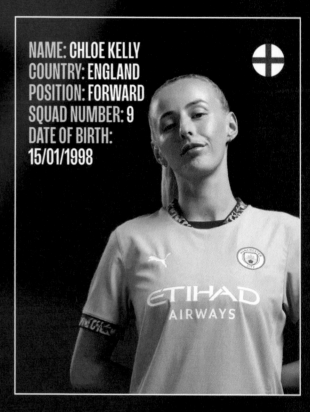

NAME: JESS PARK
COUNTRY: ENGLAND
POSITION: FORWARD
SQUAD NUMBER: 16
DATE OF BIRTH:
21/10/2001

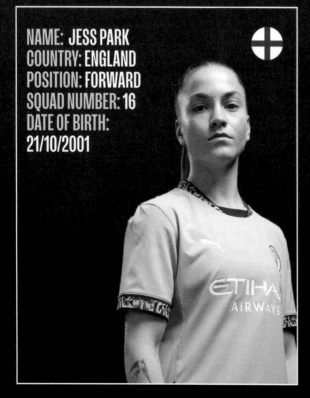

NAME: VIVIANNE MIEDEMA
COUNTRY: NETHERLANDS
COUNTRY: FORWARD
SQUAD NUMBER: 6
DATE OF BIRTH:
15/07/1996

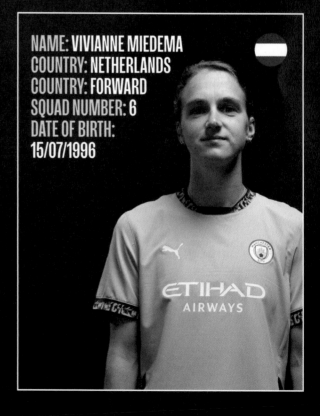

NAME: AOBA FUJINO
COUNTRY: JAPAN
POSITION: FORWARD
SQUAD NUMBER: 20
DATE OF BIRTH:
27/01/2004

NAME: MARY FOWLER
COUNTRY: AUSTRALIA
POSITION: FORWARD
SQUAD NUMBER: 8
DATE OF BIRTH:
14/02/2003

NAME: LAUREN HEMP
COUNTRY: ENGLAND
POSITION: FORWARD
SQUAD NUMBER: 11
DATE OF BIRTH:
07/08/2000

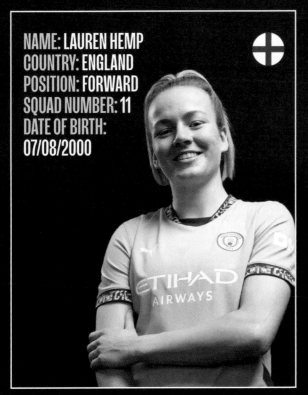

NAME: KHADIJA SHAW
COUNTRY: JAMAICA
POSITION: STRIKER
SQUAD NUMBER: 21
DATE OF BIRTH:
31/01/1997

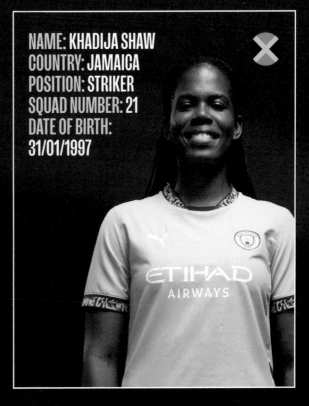

NAME: EDERSON MORAES
POSITION: GOALKEEPER
SQUAD NUMBER: 31

DATE OF BIRTH: 17/08/1993
PREVIOUS CLUBS: RIBEIRAO, RIO AVE, BENFICA

TOTAL CITY CAREER:
PLAYED: 332 **GOALS:** 0

NAME: SCOTT CARSON
POSITION: GOALKEEPER
SQUAD NUMBER: 33

DATE OF BIRTH: 03/09/1985
PREVIOUS CLUBS: LEEDS UNITED, LIVERPOOL, SHEFFIELD WEDNESDAY (LOAN), CHARLTON ATHLETIC (LOAN), ASTON VILLA (LOAN), WEST BROM, BURSASPOR, WIGAN ATHLETIC, DERBY COUNTY

TOTAL CITY CAREER:
PLAYED: 2 **GOALS:** 0

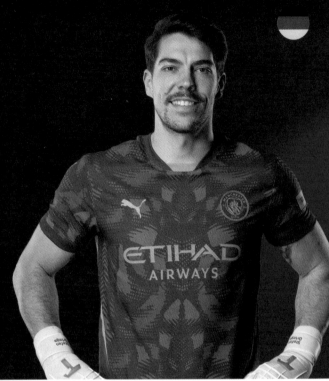

NAME: STEFAN ORTEGA MORENO
POSITION: GOALKEEPER
SQUAD NUMBER: 18

DATE OF BIRTH: 06/11/1992
PREVIOUS CLUBS: ARMINIA BIELEFELD, 1860 MUNICH

TOTAL CITY CAREER:
PLAYED: 34 **GOALS:** 0

NAME: RUBEN DIAS
POSITION: CENTRAL DEFENDER
SQUAD NUMBER: 3

DATE OF BIRTH: 14/05/1997
PREVIOUS CLUBS: BENFICA

TOTAL CITY CAREER:
PLAYED: 178 **GOALS:** 4

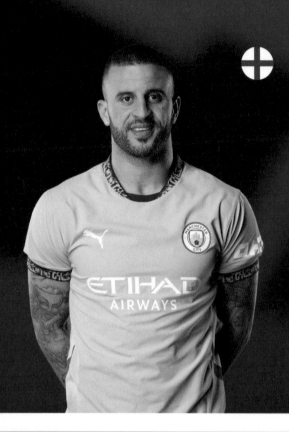

NAME: KYLE WALKER
POSITION: RIGHT-BACK
SQUAD NUMBER: 2

DATE OF BIRTH: 28/05/1990
PREVIOUS CLUBS: SHEFFIELD UNITED, NORTHAMPTON (LOAN), SPURS, SHEFFIELD UNITED (LOAN), QPR (LOAN), ASTON VILLA (LOAN)

TOTAL CITY CAREER:
PLAYED: 301 GOALS: 6

NAME: MANUEL AKANJI
POSITION: DEFENDER
SQUAD NUMBER: 25

DATE OF BIRTH: 19/07/1995
PREVIOUS CLUBS: FC WINTERTHUR, FC BASEL, BORUSSIA DORTMUND

TOTAL CITY CAREER:
PLAYED: 96 GOALS: 5

NAME: JOHN STONES
POSITION: CENTRAL DEFENDER
SQUAD NUMBER: 5

DATE OF BIRTH: 28/05/1994
PREVIOUS CLUBS: BARNSLEY, EVERTON

TOTAL CITY CAREER:
PLAYED: 257 **GOALS:** 16

NAME: JOSKO GVARDIOL
POSITION: DEFENDER
SQUAD NUMBER: 24

DATE OF BIRTH: 23/01/2002
PREVIOUS CLUBS: DINAMO ZAGREB, RB LEIPZIG

TOTAL CITY CAREER:
PLAYED: 42 **GOALS:** 5

NAME: NATHAN AKE
POSITION: DEFENDER
SQUAD NUMBER: 6

DATE OF BIRTH: 18/02/1995
PREVIOUS CLUBS: CHELSEA, READING (LOAN), WATFORD (LOAN), BOURNEMOUTH

TOTAL CITY CAREER:
PLAYED: 125 GOALS: 10

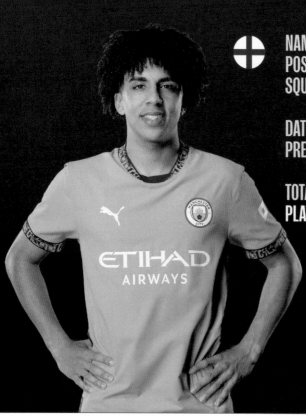

NAME: RICO LEWIS
POSITION: DEFENDER/MIDFIELDER
SQUAD NUMBER: 82

DATE OF BIRTH: 21/11/2004
PREVIOUS CLUBS: NONE

TOTAL CITY CAREER:
PLAYED: 50 GOALS: 3

*STATS CORRECT AT END OF 23/24 SEASON

NAME: ILKAY GÜNDOĞAN
POSITION: MIDFIELDER
SQUAD NUMBER: 19

DATE OF BIRTH: 24/10/1990
PREVIOUS CLUBS: VFL BOCHUM II, 1. FC NURNBERG, BORUSSIA DORTMUND, MANCHESTER CITY, BARCELONA

TOTAL CITY CAREER:
PLAYED: 305 GOALS: 60

NAME: OSCAR BOBB
POSITION: MIDFIELDER
SQUAD NUMBER: 52

DATE OF BIRTH: 12/07/2003
PREVIOUS CLUBS: NONE

TOTAL CITY CAREER:
PLAYED: 26 GOALS: 2

NAME: RODRIGO
POSITION: DEFENSIVE MIDFIELDER
SQUAD NUMBER: 16

DATE OF BIRTH: 22/06/1996
PREVIOUS CLUBS: VILLARREAL B, VILLARREAL, ATLÉTICO MADRID

TOTAL CITY CAREER:
PLAYED: 257 **GOALS:** 26

NAME: MATHEUS NUNES
POSITION: MIDFIELDER
SQUAD NUMBER: 27

DATE OF BIRTH: 27/08/1998
PREVIOUS CLUBS: ESTORIL, SPORTING CP, WOLVERHAMPTON WANDERERS

TOTAL CITY CAREER:
PLAYED: 28 **GOALS:** 0

*STATS CORRECT AT END OF 23/24 SEASON

NAME: JEREMY DOKU
POSITION: MIDFIELDER
SQUAD NUMBER: 11

DATE OF BIRTH: 27/05/2002
PREVIOUS CLUBS: R.S.C. ANDERLECHT, RENNES

TOTAL CITY CAREER:
PLAYED: 43 GOALS: 6

NAME: MATEO KOVACIC
POSITION: DEFENSIVE MIDFIELDER
SQUAD NUMBER: 8

DATE OF BIRTH: 06/05/1994
PREVIOUS CLUBS: DINAMO ZAGREB, INTER MILAN, REAL MADRID, CHELSEA

TOTAL CITY CAREER:
PLAYED: 46 GOALS: 3

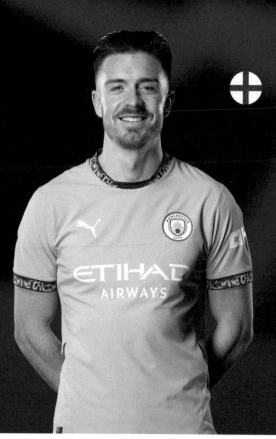

NAME: JACK GREALISH
POSITION: WINGER
SQUAD NUMBER: 10

DATE OF BIRTH: 10/09/1995
PREVIOUS CLUBS: ASTON VILLA, NOTTS COUNTY (LOAN)

TOTAL CITY CAREER:
PLAYED: 125 **GOALS:** 14

NAME: KEVIN DE BRUYNE
POSITION: ATTACKING MIDFIELDER
SQUAD NUMBER: 17

DATE OF BIRTH: 28/06/1991
PREVIOUS CLUBS: GENK, CHELSEA, WERDER BREMEN (LOAN), WOLFSBURG

TOTAL CITY CAREER:
PLAYED: 382 **GOALS:** 102

NAME: PHIL FODEN
POSITION: MIDFIELDER
SQUAD NUMBER: 47

DATE OF BIRTH: 28/05/2000
PREVIOUS CLUBS: NONE

TOTAL CITY CAREER:
PLAYED: 270 GOALS: 87

NAME: BERNARDO SILVA
POSITION: ATTACKING MIDFIELDER
SQUAD NUMBER: 20

DATE OF BIRTH: 10/08/1994
PREVIOUS CLUBS: BENFICA, MONACO

TOTAL CITY CAREER:
PLAYED: 355 GOALS: 67

*STATS CORRECT AT END OF 23/24 SEASON

NAME: SAVINHO
POSITION: ATTACKING MIDFIELDER
SQUAD NUMBER: 26

DATE OF BIRTH: 10/04/2004
PREVIOUS CLUBS: GIRONA, ATLÉTICO MINEIRO, TROYES, JONG PSV, PSV

TOTAL CITY CAREER:
PLAYED: 0 GOALS: 0

NAME: ERLING HAALAND
POSITION: STRIKER
SQUAD NUMBER: 9

DATE OF BIRTH: 21/07/2000
PREVIOUS CLUBS: BRYNE FK, MOLDE, RED BULL SALZBURG, BORUSSIA DORTMUND

TOTAL CITY CAREER:
PLAYED: 98 GOALS: 90

*STATS CORRECT AT END OF 23/24 SEASON

WHO OWNS THESE BOOTS?

Below are six boots worn by City players last season – if you look closely, you might see one or two clues – or maybe you just know already! One clue – they could be from either our men's or women's team, good luck!

QUIZANSWERS

WORDSEARCH #1 (From page 12)

K	I	Z	R	O	D	R	I	G	O	U	B	B	G
O	D	Q	E	S	W	E	D	E	R	S	O	N	W
V	F	J	H	V	T	E	Q	F	B	U	V	B	Z
A	G	I	S	A	L	R	G	E	O	G	E	U	G
C	R	D	E	E	A	F	L	Y	X	D	O	O	V
I	E	D	O	K	U	L	C	E	E	T	E	C	A
C	A	T	B	F	R	Q	A	X	G	G	R	N	R
L	L	N	O	J	Y	W	N	N	C	C	A	H	D
E	I	W	A	L	K	E	R	D	B	S	X	I	I
A	S	C	K	O	Y	S	T	O	N	E	S	Q	O
L	H	A	O	F	G	L	M	F	K	G	C	L	L
Q	Y	D	B	I	Q	M	O	J	E	G	S	F	A
T	L	I	D	D	Z	M	M	M	E	V	J	F	F
E	D	E	P	B	N	E	C	C	I	F	H	S	V

MAN CITY WOMEN QUIZ
(From page 13)

1. C – 21
2. D – Steph Houghton
3. C – 14
4. A – Netherlands
5. B – West Ham
6. C – England to Scotland
7. A – Joie Stadium
8. D – 7,108
9. A -10
10. B – Arsenal

GUESS WHO? (From page 20)

1 - ERLING HAALAND 2 - RICO LEWIS
3 - EDERSON 4 - OSCAR BOBB

BIG CITY QUIZ
(From pages 30-33)

1. Erling Haaland
2. Fluminense
3. Cole Palmer
4. B - 149
5. Bunny Shaw
6. A - Luton Town
7. B - Welsh
8. True - in 2016, 2022 and 2024
9. Phil Foden
10. True
11. Newcastle United
12. Leeds United
13. 14
14. Leeds
15. RB Leipzig
16. True
17. One v Sevilla - lost against Arsenal and Real Madrid
18. Rico Lewis
19. B - Real Sociedad
20. Phil Foden
21. Arsenal
22. Enzo Maresca
23. C - Kevin De Bruyne
24. C - 10
25. B - 2 points
26. A - 18
27. Lauren Hemp
28. Maine Road
29. John Stones
30. The Spider
31. Borussia Dortmund
32. Mateo Kovacic
33. Mary Fowler
34. False - both ended 1-1
35. Akanji and Rodrigo
36. Didn't score a goal for City
37. Rodrigo
38. Jamaica
39. Spurs
40. B - 2

SPOT THE BALL
(From page 21)

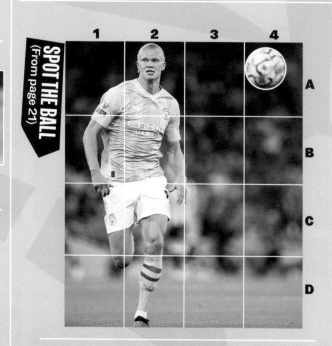

SPOT THE DIFFERENCE (From page 25)

1 - Missing 'F' for Fifa logo
2 - Missing '2023'
3 - Missing City badge on shorts
4 - Missing CWC FIFA logo
5 - Table pattern colour change
6 - Missing CWC FIFA logo

GUESS WHO?
(From page 34)

1 - RUBEN DIAS 2 - JEREMY DOKU
3 - KEVIN DE BRUYNE 4 - STEFAN ORTEGA MORENO

WORDSEARCH #2
(From page 35)

Y	B	S	F	J	T	T	F	V	K	E	L	L	Y
U	G	Y	T	D	J	G	Z	P	E	X	R	T	H
Z	P	Z	H	R	C	V	V	A	A	A	C	O	M
G	N	M	Z	A	O	F	Y	R	T	Y	A	W	U
Q	F	Q	Q	A	S	O	A	K	I	I	S	B	G
Q	G	G	J	T	K	E	R	Z	N	U	P	Y	J
U	E	B	R	O	G	A	G	D	G	R	A	X	M
P	A	E	S	E	M	P	I	A	B	Y	R	V	T
R	F	O	W	L	E	R	Y	N	W	P	I	H	W
A	D	O	A	Y	K	N	K	R	N	A	J	H	D
G	A	C	L	W	Z	M	W	T	W	U	E	E	M
D	J	C	M	S	W	K	H	O	I	O	W	M	V
O	V	W	X	E	P	X	C	F	O	B	S	P	E
Y	C	P	S	H	A	W	X	H	A	D	F	W	Z

MYSTERY GOAL SCORER! (From page 38)

KEVIN DE BRUYNE

JULIAN ALVAREZ

JOSKO GVARDIOL

PHIL FODEN

TRUE OR FALSE? (From page 39)

01.	TRUE
02.	TRUE
03.	FALSE
04.	TRUE
05.	FALSE
06.	FALSE
07.	TRUE
08.	TRUE
09.	TRUE
10.	FALSE

WHOSE BOOTS? (From page 59)

1 - EDERSON 2 - ALEX GREENWOOD
3 - OSCAR BOBB 4 - KYLE WALKER

WHERE'S RICO?

Our popular Academy graduate Rico Lewis is somewhere among the City fans celebrating another Premier League title – your job is to find him! Warning – you may need a magnifying glass!